Connie's Gifts - Interactive Books
and Collectibles
Got Challenges?
Book 3

How to: Deal when you Think you Cannot Deal

**Some helpful tips to assist you in the right Direction.
(Includes practice skills, exercises and worksheets for learning, teaching and growth).**

Offering Support for Individuals dealing with day-to-day struggles, Parents, Teachers, Counselors and Helping Professionals working with individuals diagnosed with Autism, Mental Health Disorders and Intellectual and Developmental Disabilities.

Before, During and After the Pandemic!

Book 3: Focuses on Improving Interpersonal Skills and Relationships with Parents, Peers and/or Significant Others!

Let's Move Forward!

Constance Jackson, M.Ed., LPC

Connie's Gifts- Interactive Books and Collectibles Got Challenges? Book 3

HOW TO: DEAL WHEN YOU THINK YOU CANNOT DEAL. SOME HELPFUL TIPS TO ASSIST YOU IN THE RIGHT DIRECTION. (INCLUDES PRACTICE SKILLS, EXERCISES AND WORKSHEETS FOR LEARNING, TEACHING AND GROWTH). SUPPORT FOR CHILDREN, PAREN

iUniverse books may be ordered through booksellers or by contacting:

iUniverse
1663 Liberty Drive
Bloomington, IN 47403
www.iuniverse.com
844-349-9409

ISBN: 978-1-6632-2496-5 (sc)
ISBN: 978-1-6632-2497-2 (e)

Library of Congress Control Number: 2022915756

Print information available on the last page.

iUniverse rev. date: 08/18/2022

Dedication

This book is dedicated to my God, my husband and my family. To my husband, Clyde Jackson, the love of my life, who has changed my life in a way I could have never imagined. You have supported all of my endeavors. You are my angel and my hero.

To my children: daughter, Freddricka Jackson and son, Burnell Neal Jr. I am blessed to have you in my life. You helped me to become a better person and mother. I adore and cherish you both, always. You gave purpose to my life. I am so grateful and proud of the adults you have become.To my son in-law, Jaqua J. and daughter-in-law, Brooklyn N. I am grateful for you, love you much.

To my siblings (and their spouses) Thank you to Denise P., Cornealious P. Jr, Norma B., Nethel P. (Lawanda) and Nina F. (Leonard). You are the ones I have always looked up to my entire life. Thank you for your support over the years and I love you forever!

To my nephews: Paul B., Marcus P., Zachary P., Dr. Christopher L., and Troy M., you are and always will be special to me. Love you forever.

To the next generation: my great-nieces and great-nephews: Denise's grandsons (Paul): Janye W., Vaelon W., and Caden W.; Denise's granddaughters (Paul): Morgan B., Madison B., and Bailee B. Nethel's granddaughters (Zachary): Ava P. and Kinley P. Aunt Connie loves you always! Keep the "Petitt" spirit, will, and determination going strong!

All honor to my paternal aunts and uncle: Lola Petitt-Fowler (Royce), Wilma Petitt-Hill (Robert), and Bishop Roy S. Petitt (Dr. Bennie P.) In loving memory of Ivory Petitt, Anna Petitt-Jones, Harrison Petitt, Nethel Petitt and Vivian Petitt-Miller (Elwood). In loving Memory of my maternal aunt, Jannie B. Rogers.

To our parents, Cornealious E. Petitt Sr. and Annie Johnson-Petitt, who I will forever love and be grateful to you both, for doing your best in raising six children. We are blessed to have the best of both of you! Rest in Peace. Last, but not least, thank you to all of my cousins and close friends. Special thanks to: Pamela R., Austin R. Isaac K. Sr., Angel K., Thelma H., Ruth S., Venus W., Alma J, Kevin J. and Akeva J. I am so proud of you and your accomplishments. Thank you and I love you, always!

I would like to thank and acknowledge some of those important individuals who were a great influence to my family and those who played a part in my childhood and development growing up: Rev. M.L. Harris & Carolyn Harris, Reatha & Edna Scarlett, C.L. Nathaniel, Nee Bee Curtis, Claudine Washington, Bertha Horton, Marjorie Owens, K.C. Curtis Sr., Mrs. Ivory Lee Mims, Mary Ella Heard Ford, Cleo Nelson, Claudine Bryant, Dolly Hughes, Bruce White, and Myrtle Malone. Teachers: Mrs. W. White, Mrs. E. Garrett and Mrs. N. Brandl.

Constance Jackson, LPC, M.Ed., Author

Special Thanks

I would like to say thank you for your interest in this book collection. Thank you to Dominique H., Daliah S., Brooklyn N., Denise P., and Norma B. for their support, expertise, and assistance with completing this book collection. Thank you, to all of my past and present professors, supervisors, colleagues and co-workers for theirsupport.

Disclaimer

This illustration is strictly for support of others and not intended to take the place of a licensed therapist, providing therapy or counseling services. As with therapy, clinicians and author cannot guarantee any specific results. Treatment success depends on you, the individual in which services are being provided. Seek medical attention from a helping professional, if at risk of harm to self or others, by contacting 911 or going to your nearest emergency room. National Suicide Prevention Lifeline: 988 and #800-273-8255.

Description of Book

As a helping professional, I dedicate my life to helping children and their family to the best of my ability, to facilitate empowerment and hope for a brighter future. During difficult times, therapy is not always the first choice and in some cases, not easily accessible. There are several reasons people hesitate about enrolling in therapy, such as the negative stigma of seeking help for mental health and mental illness, cost, lack of compatibility with therapist, location, insurance issues and now due to social distancing, during the Covid-19 and Coronavirus Pandemic.

This interactive book was written with the aim of supporting those individuals who are supporting others. Additionally, it's focus is to help individuals, parents and helping professionals in need of support, when dealing with day-to-day issues and with assisting others (e.g., children, teenagers and adults) that are dealing with mental health conditions and challenging behaviors. During this time of the Covid-19 Pandemic, this book offers support to those who are unable to go into an office, for face-to-face visits and those who are unfamiliar with working with said population. This interactive book is intended to help and support those who are having difficulties managing their thoughts, behavior and emotions, while coping with life changes, stressful situations, mental health conditions and IDD challenges.

This book or any therapy services cannot guarantee any specific results, outcomes or promises, but may facilitate you and/ or your family member(s), to tap into your own power and strengths, to reach personal goals.

Everything you need is within you! This illustration contains demonstrates and describes some activities and exercises that can be used in the schools, home and community settings to begin the process of self-awareness, healing and moving forward.

Therapy is about self-awareness and developing coping skills to navigate through life's challenges. Being a helping professional, for thirty-five plus years, I realized I do not have the physical capacity to work endless hours, to help all of the children and families I would love to help. By writing this book, I can share some of the information and techniques that I have learned, used and acquired over the years. Some have proven helpful in assisting hundreds of children, families and adults. For me, this book is like my version of the story of "Saving the Starfish." If I can help one, maybe I can make a difference in one person's life and even for the next generation. My version of the story is not helping people, one by one, but putting these skills into a written form, to share with all of those in need, simultaneously, maybe even around the world. I hope this information reaches you. Remember, there is always hope!

About the Author

Constance Jackson is a Licensed Professional Counselor, who completed a Master's Degree in Education, Specializing in Community Counseling and successfully passed the National Counseling Exam (NCE). She is qualified to counsel under the guidelines of Texas States Board of Examiners of Professional Counselors. Her formal education was received at University of Houston- Main and University of Houston- Victoria. Work experience includes the following facilities: Schools, Day Programs, Community Centers, and Hospitals (Inpatient and Out-patient settings). She has helped hundreds of individual and families through conducting individual, group, family and couple's therapy.

Work Experience

As of 2021, Counselor Jackson has worked 36 years in Mental Health/ Intellectual and Development Disabilities (MH/ IDD) Services. She has worked in private practice, various health care settings as a Direct Care Staff, Behavior Intervention Specialist, Voc. Habilitation Manager, Counselor/Therapist, Clinical Treatment Director of a Residential Treatment Center, all with the purpose of supporting and assisting individuals and their families. Lastly, Counselor Jackson has experience working with persons of varied ethnic, racial, sexual orientation, and religious backgrounds. One of her goals is to aid those she can help, when others have turned them away. Her moto is, "If I do not help, who will. So, I will try." So many people are in pain, some due to past and present events. Some have been harmed through generational trauma. There is hope through intervention (e.g., psychoeducation and access to resources) and helping children, parents and their family, to develop steps to achieve their personal and family goals.

x

Theories of Counseling

Counselor Jackson adheres to a combination of three frameworks of theories: Cognitive Behavior Therapy (CBT), Rational Emotive Behavior Therapy (REBT), and Solution Focus. For CBT, developed by Dr. Aaron Beck, focuses on the interconnection of your thoughts, behavior and feelings and how they affect the other. The goal is to reframe those thoughts for a more positive perspective. 2). The Rational emotive behavior therapy (REBT) approach to counseling, focuses on the here and now, and not past or future events, but refuting irrational thoughts and beliefs. (REBT) also focuses on educational and learning processes. Learning or teaching individuals new thoughts and behaviors patterns, resulting in possible resolution to the problem that brought you here today. 3). and the Solution- Focus realm, developed by Shazer and Berg. This technique may be used to reinforce successes and assist the client in gaining self-confidence and self-awareness with a clear focus of the client being the expert over their lives, and working within their own story; working to assist individuals to find alternatives to a more fulfilling life (Shazer & Berg). The goal of therapy and this illustration is to assist individuals to reach self-awareness through an evidence-based approach. In this illustration the author will provide you with additional information, concrete examples and interactive exercises, that will hopefully assist you with challenging behaviors in the home, school and communicating settings, if consistently applied. This illustration does not make guarantees, but may offer some guidance, support and hope by developing potential alternatives to reach personal goals.

Note

Book Instructions: In this book, functional coping skills will be underlined, to indirectly provide guidance and prompts to functional alternatives to manage challenging and difficult situations and behaviors. It also includes positive affirmations, at the beginning of each exercise, to increase self-confidence, and self-worth. There are notes, examples, narratives and instructions provided for guidance as you complete each exercise. Be empowered to mindfully implement some of these healthy alternatives and coping skills into your daily living. A certificate of completion is available at the end of the book for learned skills.

My Note Page

_____

_____

_____

_____

_____

_____

_____

_____

_____

_____

_____

_____

_____

_____

_____

_____

_____

_____

Journal your thoughts.

Contents

You are a Superstar! _____

Managing Anger as a Coping Skill!

Anger is sometimes a secondary emotion. If you can manage or resolve the first emotion, you can manage your anger.

Question: Can you identify your primary emotions that trigger your angry feelings? Examples: fear, sadness, disrespect, disappointment, anxiety, etc.

Example/ Illustration: The taxi cab driver was late for work and was afraid of getting fired. BJ is driving down the highway, relaxed and listening to his favorite music.

At that moment, the taxi cab driver cuts B. J. off in traffic, almost causing an accident. His negative thoughts cause him to stomp his gas, and shake his fist.

He starts breathing hard, with a racing heartbeat (body cues). Then he yells, "You jerk, move out of my way!" Now, he is angry!"

Question. What was his first emotion? Answer here. _____.

Question. What was his second emotion? Answer here. _____.

Exercise: Look at the list below. What are some emotions you feel before you become angry?

Circle the one that applies: (e.g., Sad, disrespected, disappointed, hungry, lonely, tired, frustrated, jealous, irritable, etc.)

Note: Anger is a normal emotion. It is what you do when you are angry that is important! Answers: (e.g., scared and angry)

Behind every Storm there is Sunshine! _____

Increase your Self-Awareness!

Let's learn to deal with your primary or first emotions, then you can better manage your anger! Yes!!

Exercise/ Question: What are some healthy ways to deal with your uncomfortable emotions?

List of healthy coping skills that you can use (e. g., communicate, use "I" statements, humor, exercise, be patient, take a break, forgive, find a solution, etc.)

The emotions that make you feel vulnerable, (e.g., scared, fearful, anxious, disappointed, depressed and frustrated) are the emotions we often want to avoid or lessen. At some point in time, it is important to process and/or talk about events that led to these emotions to manage and overcome them.

Example/ Exercise: Below, identify and explore each emotion, prior to feeling angry.

1. Churchwell was disappointed that his friend stood him up, instead of getting angry, what is a better alternative?
    "Churchwell was disappointed, so he_____."
2. Now, write down a situation, in which you became __(Disappointed)___, and then you became angry.
    "Once I was disappointed when_____."
3. Write down a situation, in which you became ___ (Disrespected) ___, and then you became angry.
    "I felt disrespect when _____   _____."
4. Write down a situation, in which you became ___ (Scared) ___, and then you became angry.
    I felt scared when _____."

Answer: (Churchwell can wait to communicate with his friend, do something else (alone or with others) or reschedule).

_____

Note: The more you can resolve and process your thoughts and emotions, the more you can manage your anger.

You are Sunshine! _____

Self-Care as a Coping Skill!

Self- Care: Is what you do to take complete care of yourself. The more you care for yourself, the more you can care for others.

Forms of self-care

Exercise I: Explore the list of activities below. Place a check mark on the designated line to identify which self-care activity you perform well.

- Physical - exercise, eat healthy, annual exam, drink water, sleep and rest _____
- Mental – manage stressors, relax, do favorite activities to increase your happiness _____
- Emotional – see therapist, journal, stay connected with family and friends _____
- Spiritual - pray, meditate, get in touch with nature_____
- Social - stay connected with peers, family, have fun each day_____
- Practical - school, learn a new skill, practice a talent, take a course, getting business in order_____

Exercise II: List the self-care activity you need to improve on, for more balance in your life.

Example: "I need to improve by physical self-care, by exercising for .30 minutes each day."

1. _____.
2. _____.
3. _____.
4. _____.
5. _____.

Note: The more you balance self-care, the more balance you will have in your life. Put yourself first!

Narration: Utilize this illustration to explore forms of self-care and self-love, as well as, having balance in your life.

Having Balance is Better! _____

Self-Love as a Coping Skill!

Love yourself by making healthy choices!

Balance is Important

Examples of self-love and self-care to facilitate balance:

- Get rest and proper sleep
- Exercise
- Eat healthy and hydrate
- Rely on support system
- Spend time with family and friends
- Study, develop new skills and do homework
- Meditate and pray
- Set Boundaries by saying "No."
- Respect boundaries
- Focus on self
- Work, be self-sufficient
- Organize time, desk, closet, and home
- Play and schedule vacation time

Note: If you do not care for yourself, properly, the scale might tip over to one side, causing self-harm. "CRASH or BURNOUT!!"

Be the Rainbow! _____

Self-Care as a Coping Skill!

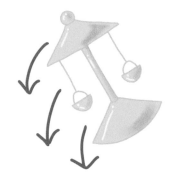

Sue lacked practical, emotional and mental self-care (e.g., reduced study/ learning, organizing, asking for help, therapy & managing stressors).

Sue overloaded social, practical and physical self-care (e.g., increased play, focus on friends, gym, work hours, partying, sleeping & relaxing).

Imbalance can cause harm!

Exercise: Using the illustration above, help Sue to answer the following questions to increase her use of self-care and self-love.

1.) Is Sue putting herself at risk of failing grades and/ or failing health? yes, or no?
Explain: _____ .

2.) Is this behavior showing self-love? Yes or No?
Explain: _____ .

3.) What can Sue do to make her life better?
Explain: _____ .

Yes! Way to Go, Sue!!

I will do it! _____

Let us revisit Healthy Boundaries as a Coping Skill!

Healthy boundaries are important to protect yourself and others. Say "no" if you really don't want to do something. When setting healthy boundaries, you cannot worry about yourself and others. You have to put yourself first.

Example: Connie asked Pam to skip class with her. Pam did not know what to do, but she skipped with Connie, because she wanted to be cool and keep their friendship.

Question/ Exercise:

1.) What do you think Pam should have done, while maintaining her friendship with Connie?
Write your answer below?

_____

_____

2.) If this were you, what would be your best choice for you and your family (e.g., skip or go to class)?
Write your answer below?

_____

_____

3.) Which choice will cause you the most problems?
Write your answer below?

_____

_____

4.) Which choice will work for you (e. g., cause you the least problems/ worry, and the most happiness and peace)? Write your answer below?

_____

_____

Note: Remember to practice self-love and do what is best for you and your support network.

Circle your answer(s): Set boundaries, end friendship, say, "no, I cannot do that." "I will see you later," walk away and/ or follow class schedule.

My Notes

_____

_____

_____

_____

_____

_____

_____

_____

_____

_____

_____

_____

_____

_____

Journal your thoughts.

Start Today! _____

Self-Awareness and Cognitive Dissonance!

Cognitive Dissonance is when one is faced with two conflicting thoughts.

I do not believe in cheating. It is dishonest.

I took the answer sheet from a friend. I needed to pass my final exam or I would fail and ruin my future! I hope no one finds out.

This conflict can produce feelings of guilt, shame, anxiety and stress, etc.

One coping skill is to match thoughts/ core beliefs, behavior and desired feelings.

Note: Pain, loss and grief can also cause cognitive dissonance. A negative or traumatic event can draw so much of your energy, time and focus, that your most basic needs may be left unattended (e.g., hygiene, education, work, meals, sleep, caring for business matters, self and of family).

Exercise: When we make unhealthy decisions (e.g., lying, stealing, cheating, hitting, gossiping, bullying, etc.), who and what is the cause of our cognitive dissonance, if the choice or behavior goes against our core beliefs?

Explore, Who? _____.

Explore, What? _____.

How would you fix it, or reduce cognitive dissonance? _____.

_____

Note: Here is a list of healthy coping skills, (e.g., challenge automatic thoughts, use mindfulness, think before acting, be congruent with thoughts/beliefs, behavior and feelings, make decisions with consequences in mind (positive and negative).

My Notes

_____
_____
_____
_____
_____
_____
_____
_____
_____
_____
_____
_____

Journal your thoughts.

Forgive and Live! _____

Children understanding Parents: Children seeing Parents as People.

As you mature, you will start to see your parents as human beings too. Be mindful, that your parents feel joy, hurt, love, and get disappointed, just as you do.

Sometimes, children think their parents are overacting, being unreasonable and even overbearing. Guess what, sometimes children are correct.

But, put yourself in your parents' shoes. Have empathy for your parents. Maybe by the end of the exercise, you will use empathy, as a coping skill to improve your relationship with your parents. Let's explore, what it feels like to be a concerned parent.

Illustration:

Parents value you as their most, valuable prized possession. This being said, for lack of a better phrase, because children are not possessions, but children are the responsibility of the parents, until they are of legal age. You are the most important thing in their world. Parents work to provide your needs and some of your wants. "Wants" are optional and should be considered a "Bonus."

So, now that we have clarified, "most prized possession," answer the following questions.

Exercise:

1). What do you value the most? _____

2). What is your "most prized possession?" _____

Note: This could be your cell phone, television, laptop, music system, game system, clothes or shoes.

Exercise: Now, Let's explore Qua's most valuable possession and see what his reaction might look like, when having thoughts of losing that item.

Example:

Qua's most valued possession is his cell phone. One day, he thought he had lost his cellphone. He felt afraid, anxious, disappointed and even angry, because he thought he had lost something important to him (e.g., personal information, contacts videos, and all of his favorite music).

My Notes

_____

_____

_____

_____

Journal your thoughts.

Narration: Continue utilizing the following illustration to facilitate improvement in relationships between parents/ adult and child/ individual being served.

Take Action!_____

Children understanding Parents: Children seeing Parents as People.

Just think, you are so valuable to your parents. Sometimes, children don't understand why parents get so upset. Your parents may feel the same way that Qua felt, when he thought he had lost his cellphone. Parents want the best for you and do not want to lose you, in the process of becoming a healthy, well-rounded adult and a contributing part of society. Remember, you matter.

Exercise/ Question: What can you do to be more understanding of your parents, when they worry about you?

Note: Earlier we discuss primary and secondary emotions. If your parents seem to be upset or angry with you, what coping skills can you use to improve your relationship? Answer here. _____.

Here are some examples to improve interpersonal skills with your parents, (e.g., Reframe your thoughts, empathy, listen, follow instructions, communicate, express your thoughts, emotions and needs, etc.).

Exercise: What are some specific things you can do, at your home, to improve your positive interaction with your parents and family members?

Answer here.

1.

2.

3.

Great Job! I am proud of you!

__Narration: Continue utilizing the following illustration, to facilitate improved relationships between parents/ adult and child/ individual being served.__

Note: Teenagers and adults can <u>generalize this information</u>/ coping skills, after the previous lesson, for their own relationships, to improve their interpersonal skills with others.

Achieve and Believe!_____

Children understanding Parents: Children seeing Parents as People.

Showing Empathy to Parents & Others

Webster defines empathy as: the feeling that you understand and share another person's experience and emotion.

Exercise: Parents value you and what do you value? See some examples below.
List three choices here. _____

cell phone	pet	watch
TV	tablet	gym
video game	favorite toy	friends

These activities listed above are also things you can do or use to make yourself happy when feeling sad or depressed. **From the list above, write five options to increase your happiness or add your own choices.** Parents/ Adults can also use the preferred items on the list, as positive reinforcements, and deliver after the child has exhibited a desired behavior. This will increase the probability of the behavior occurring more frequently in the future.

1.
2.
3.
4.
5.

What can children and parents do to reinforce desired behavior in each other? To start, "A "thank you" and/ or a "I love you!" is always welcomed and appreciated.

Trust in yourself! _____

Reciprocity as a Coping Skill! Giving mutual respect to each other.

Note: To increase interpersonal skills and positive interaction with parents and others, it is essential to demonstrate reciprocity. Reciprocity does not just involve material items or money. Reciprocity can be a mutual exchange of time, support, a helping hand, respect or just a listening ear.

Exercise. Let's explore what reciprocity looks like when interacting with others. According to the chart below, determine which relationship would be best for you? Select relationship 1 or 2?

#1: Healthy Relationship	#2: Unhealthy Relationship
Give (→) Take (←)	Give (→) Take (←)
→	→
←	→
→	→
←	→
→	→
→	←
←	→
←	→
→	→
←	→
←	←
Does this relationship demonstrate reciprocity? Yes or No	Does this relationship demonstrate reciprocity? Yes or No

Question/Exercise:

1. Which relationship would you prefer?

_____

2. Identify a person or current relationship you have with someone. Identify if you are the giver or the taker in that relationship.
   Write the identified person here. _____

3. List the people, in which you have a healthy relationship. List three or more relationships that resemble the relationship in column #1.
   1.
   2.
   3.

4. List the people, in which you have an unhealthy relationship. List three or more relationships that resemble the relationship in column #2.
   1.
   2.
   3.

5. Are your parents on the healthy side or the unhealthy side? Circle your answer: healthy OR unhealthy

6. What can you do to improve relationships with other people?

_____

My Notes

_____

_____

_____

_____

_____

_____

_____

_____

_____

_____

_____

_____

_____

_____

_____

_____

_____

_____

Journal your thoughts.

True treasures are within! _____

Self-Motivation as a Coping Skill.

Self-awareness: What Motivates your behavior?
There are often five motives for exhibiting behaviors. See examples below:
1. To get <u>attention</u> (e.g., from teacher, parent, friend).
2. To get something/ a <u>tangible item</u> (e. g., toy, candy, prize, money).
3. To <u>avoid</u> something, you do not like (e.g., chores, people, places, things).
4. To <u>escape</u> something aversive (e.g., dishes, hunger, thirst, heat, cold, places, people).
5. It is <u>self-stimulating</u> or it feels good, soothes (e.g., shake legs, tap fingers, rock body, flap hands, and/ or could feel exciting or entertaining).

Now, self-examine. Why do we exhibit certain behaviors? Below, write your motive beside each behavior. Note: Generalize this information for other behaviors, to increase your self-awareness.

Raise my hand in class? _____.
Say hello? _____.
Drink water? _____.
Tantrum?_____.
Kick? _____.
Scream? _____.
Cursing?_____.
Hit? _____.
Be nice? _____.

Exercise: After exploring and determining your motives. Identify/ develop healthy and prosocial coping skills that will better work for you, to get the same desired outcome.
1.
2.
3.

Narration: Continue to utilize this illustration to increase your self-awareness and recognize the motives for your behavior. Then, discover healthy coping skills to meet your needs.

You are the best! _____

Self-Motivation as a Coping Skill.

Example:

Negative Coping Skills:	Pro-Social and Healthy Coping Skills:
Yell, scream, or cry for no apparent reason	Talk calmly
Kick	Communicate
Refuse to follow instructions. Say, "It is too hard."	Ask for help

Exercise: Identify and write down negative coping skills you have used to get your way or get out of something.
    1.
    2.
    3.

Now, find a healthy way to meet your needs and wants.
    1.
    2.
    3.

Answer: raise hand- attention, drink water- tangible item, scream- avoid

Narration: Use this exercise to see the positive qualities in others (e.g., parents, family members, helping professionals, teachers, partners, friends, etc).

You are the Best! _____

Recognize the positive qualities you see in others, as a coping skill!

Exercise.

1). Identify and list an important person in your life.

2). Write name here. "_____ is important to me."

3). Now, see the list below and put a check mark by each positive quality you see in that person. (Check all that apply. Add more if applicable.)

helpful _	funny _	giving _
encouraging _	smart _	outgoing _
responsible _	adventurous _	takes care of business _
hopeful _	brave _	care giver _
loving _	valuable _	advocate _
caring _	kind _	
hard-working _	strong _	

Challenge. One time a day, tell someone that they did something good.

Example: Children give compliments to adults and adults give compliments to children. The pendulum swings both ways on a clock, as well as, in relationships.

Practice Reciprocity!

Be Optimistic! _____

Recognize the positive qualities you see in the child or individual served, as a coping skill!

For Parents, Adults, and Helping Professional(s): Seeing the positives in your child or youth may stop the cycle of only seeing the negative behavior that they exhibit. Focus on the positives and you will probably see more positives.

Exercise.

1). Identify and list the child or youth. Write name here. "_____ has positive qualities."

2). Now, see the list below and put a check mark by each positive quality you recognize. (Check all that apply. Add more if applicable.)

awesome _	responsible _	trustworthy _
encouraging _	funny _	positive _
responsible _	smart _	helpful _
fun _	brave _	hard-working _
loving _	valuable _	adventurous _
caring _	kind _	giving _

Note: The things you focus on the most will increase! Wow, the sky is the limit for you and your child/ family! Practice recognizing the good! Challenge: At least, three times a day, <u>be mindful</u> to tell your child/ individual good things.

**Narration: Use this exercise to increase self-awareness and to be your authentic self.**

I appreciate You! _____

Increase Self-Awareness, as a Coping Skill!

Exercise: Inside Face ---> Outside Face

Note: We all have coping skills to protect ourselves. Sometimes, we display an, outside face, as a mask to cover up our vulnerable emotions. We may show an angry face, but our, inside face, may be scared, anxious or even sad. There are faces we show to others (Outside face), that may be totally different, from the (Inside face), of how we feel inside. The more we become our authentic selves, the more those faces will become similar. Let's identify your (Inside and Outside) Face. The face that you show to others when feeling vulnerable. The closer you get to becoming your true self/ your authentic you, the more you will be at peace with yourself and others. (Let's gain a sense of self).

Let's explore your Inside and Outside face:

Example: I am afraid the teacher will call on me in class.

The face I Show to Others --->

Note: The motivation or purpose for making this angry face (e.g., escape and avoidance of an adverse situation).

Exercise. Draw your Outside Face below.

<table>
<tr>
<td>

</td>
<td>

If I display an angry face,
maybe she/he will
not call on me.
I do not want others to
know I am scared or that I
do not know the answer.
Behavior- "No, I'm not doing it!"

</td>
</tr>
</table>

Question: Have you ever pretended to be angry to avoid something or someone? Answer. Yes or No.

Note: It is difficult to be happy, when you have to pretend to be angry. Why be afraid, just try. If you are lacking a skill (e.g., reading, math, social skills, communication, etc.), just practice, learn, study each day and you will get better. We all have a weakness. Do not feel down or sorry for yourself. You are stronger than you think!

Be empowered! Take Action! You can do it! Believe!

My Notes

_____

_____

_____

_____

_____

_____

Journal your thoughts.

__Narration:__ Continue to use this exercise to increase self-awareness and to be your authentic self.

Increase Self-Awareness, as a Coping Skill!

Exercise: Inside Face ---> Outside Face

The face I do not show others --->   "I'm scared inside."

Exercise. Let's explore your Inside and Outside face:

Exercise. Draw your Inside and Outside Face. Identify the Emotion? What is the Function or Purpose of your behavior?

Outside Face: The face I Show to Others ---> **Inside Face:** The face I Do not Show Others --->

Exercise. Identify the Emotion: _____, Identify Purpose of behavior_____.

Self-Acceptance! _____

Self- Awareness as a Coping Skill!

Note 1: Find healthy coping skills, to be your true self, your authentic you. Examples: (e. g., ask for help, take action, study, be prepared, challenge negative thoughts, positive self-talk).

Note 2: You deserve self-love. You should not have to show anger, as a coping skill. Learn healthy coping skills, so you can be happy and live to your fullest potential.

My Notes

_____
_____
_____
_____
_____
_____
_____
_____
_____
_____
_____
_____
_____
_____
_____
_____
_____

Journal your thoughts.

Reach for the Stars! _____

Self-Acceptance as a Coping Skill!

Find Your Authentic Self

As you learn more about yourself and about the world around you, you will develop a sense of self. So, do not be afraid to try new things and have new experiences. Being your authentic self, occurs when your inside and your outside face become more alike or similar, regardless of the people and/ or places, in which you encounter.

Be your authentic self! You are good enough!

Inside Face	Outside Face

I am happy inside.	I am happy, but afraid the teacher will call on me. I can still be happy, work through my fears, challenge my negative thoughts and use self-talk, "I studied. I will try." Guess what? "I did it! I got the correct answer!"

Examples of challenging negative thoughts. "They might laugh at me, but no big deal."

Replacement/Alternate thoughts: <u>I will try</u>! I have an opportunity to learn! Yes! I did it!

Follow your own path! _____

Positive Reinforcement!

Exercise. Make Your Positive Reinforcement List.

How to make a positive reinforcement list. Spread out select or favorite items, in front of the individual. These should be preferred favors. Allow the individual to select prefer items, 1 by 1, from most favorite to least favorite. You may also present items in pairs. Additionally, you may ask the individual, for verbal responses or ask their significant other of preferred items.

Make a list 1-10. You can implement a positive reinforcement procedure, by delivering preferred items/ activities after desired behaviors. Reinforcers may change and vary, due to age and situations.

Name: _____ Date:

Positive Reinforcers
1.
2.
3.
4.
5.
6.
7.
8.
9.
10.

You did It!
You completed Book III

Narration: As we come to the end of book three, let us continue to focus on self-awareness and healthy coping skills. Complete a summary of what you have learned overall from completing book three. Remember to review skills, if necessary, retain handouts and worksheets as a reference for future use, and practice of learned skills.

You are one of a kind. Embrace it! _____

Be your Authentic Self

Summary of Part III

Note: Challenge thoughts that make you feel depressed, sad, have low self-confidence, low self-esteem, feel lonely or alone.

Self-Love is key. You deserve to be happy. Be mindful to make decisions that make you happy, not unhappy (e.g., do homework, study, follow rules, work, be independent, listen, be on time, etc.).

You have finished Book 3. Overall, what did you learn about yourself?

1.
2.
3.

What are some healthy coping skills that will work for you and others around you?

1.
2.
3.

How is your self-awareness!

Write a Note to self on what you have learned about yourself, while completing Book III.

_____

_____

Narration: Parents, individuals and helping professionals may present this Certificate of Achievement for completion of Book Three, if skills were learned and can be implemented, as noted in the summary. Hopefully, some of the skills learned have helped the child or individual to improve their self-awareness, quality of life, and developed coping skills to assist with regulating thoughts, behavior and mood. Remember, there is no quick fix, when seeking change. It is a process. Hang in there for the process. You are worth it!

Certificate:

Hero Award!!
Certificate of Achievement
Awarded to:

_____

For the completion of Connie's Gifts - Interactive Books and Collectibles
3 of 3

Great job on Increasing Self-Awareness and Being Brave Enough to be You! You are a true Hero!

Sign:_____ Date:_____

Title:_____

Subject Index, Terms, & Definitions

Table of Content: Subject Index/ Reference for Book Content: - Book III:

Terms/ Definitions

Absolute thoughts. The tendency to think in concrete, black and white terms. (Oxford Dictionary)

Automatic thoughts. Personalized notions that are triggered by particular stimuli that lead to emotional responses. (Corey, G., 2009, p. 288)

Backwards Chaining/ Learning. Behavior linked together beginning with learning the last behavior in the sequence. (J. Cooper,2007, p436, 443)

Behavior. Acts, habits, and reactions that are observable and measurable. (Corey, G., 2009, p. 253

Challenging/Disrupting irrational beliefs. The most common cognitive method of REBT consists of the therapist actively disputing individual's irrational beliefs and teaching them how to do this challenging on their own. (Corey, G., 2009, p. 282)

Cognition. The act or process of knowing, perception. (Corey, G., 2009, p. 253). Insight, philosophies, ideas, opinions, self-talk, and judgements, that constitute one's fundamental values, attitudes and belief

Cognitive Behavior Therapy/ CBT. Aaron T. Beck founded cognitive therapy, which gives a primary tole to thinking as it influences behavior. (Corey, G., 2009, p. 9)

Cognitive Distortions. An exaggerated or irrational thought pattern involved in the onset or perpetuation of psychopathological states, such as depression and anxiety. Thoughts that cause individuals to perceive realty inaccurately. (Beck, J. S. 2011)

Cognitive Triangle. Proposed by Aaron Beck. A diagram that depicts how our thoughts, emotions and behavior are all interconnected with each other and influences one another. (Cully, J.A., & Teten, A.L. 2008)

Cognitive Restructuring. Is a central technique of cognitive therapy that teaches people how to improve themselves by replacing faulty cognition with constructive beliefs. Involves helping individual learn to monitor their self-talk, identify maladaptive self-talk and substitute adaptive self-talk for their negative self-talk. (Corey, G., 2009, p. 278/ Ellis,2003)

Coping skills. To acquire more effective strategies in dealing with stressful situations. (Corey, G., 2009, p.297).

Dysfunctional. (coping skills). Not operating normally or properly. (Oxford Dictionary) Unhealthy coping mechanism that bring temporary relief, joy, feeling of numbness for pain.

Forward Chaining/Learning. Behavior linked together beginning with learning the first behavior in the sequence. (J. Cooper,2007, p. 442)

Functional. (coping skills). Having a special activity, purpose, or task relating to the way in which something works or operate. (Oxford Dictionary) Permits an individual to deal directly with the stressor faced.

Generalize. To apply a behavior or skill to other conditions of interest. (J. Cooper, 2007, p. 196)

Interconnected. To connect with one another. (Oxford Dictionary)

Internalize. To keep or take something in. It can be used in either a positive or negative way. (Merriam-Webster Dictionary)

Interpersonal Skills. Relating to relationships or communication between people. (Oxford dictionary)

Intervention. Action taken to improve a situation, especially a medical disorder (Oxford Language)

Mindfulness. The process that involves becoming increasingly observant and aware of external and internal stimuli in the present moment and adopting an open attitude toward accepting what is rather than judging the current situation. (Corey, G., 2009, p. 255)

Normalization. Refers to the use of progressively more typical environment, expectations, and procedures "to establish and/or maintain personal behavior which are as culturally normal as possible." (J. Cooper, 2007, p. 59)

Positive Affirmations. Defined as positive phrases or statements that we repeat to ourselves. Generally, they are used to manifest goals, dreams or experiences we desire. (Szente, J. 2007)

Positive Reinforcement. Occurs when a response is followed immediately by the presentation of a stimulus and, as a result, similar responses occur more frequently in the future. (J. Cooper, 2007, p. 258)

Psychoeducation. Premised on the idea that education is about changing perceptions as well as acquiring knowledge. Gladding, S.T. (2012).

Psychotherapy. Is a process of engagement between two persons, both of whom are bound to change through the therapeutic venture. At best a collaborative process that involves both the therapist and individual in co-constructing solutions to concerns. The counselor facilitates healing through a process of genuine dialogue with the individual. (Corey, G, 2009 p. 6)

Rational Emotive Behavior therapy/ REBT. Albert Ellis founded (REBT). A highly didactic, cognitive, action-oriented model of therapy that stresses the role of thinking and belief systems as the root of personal problems. (Corey, G., 2009, p. 9)

Reality Therapy. Focuses on individuals' current behavior and stresses developing clear plans for new behaviors. Like reality therapy, behavior therapy puts a premium on doing and on taking steps to make concrete changes. (Corey, G, 2009 p. 10)

Reframe. Putting what is known into a new, mor useful perspective. (Corey, G., 2009, p. 421)

Replacement behavior. Determining an adaptive behavior that will take the place of another. (J. Cooper,2007, p. 60)

Role playing. Role playing has emotive, cognitive, and behavioral components, and the therapist often interrupts to show clients what they are telling themselves to create their disturbances and what they can do to change their unhealthy feelings to healthy ones. (Corey, G p. 284)

Self-Care. When a person looks after their own basic health needs, without needing anyone else to help them. (Collin dictionary)

Self-Evaluate. The process or an instance of assessing oneself and weighing up one's achievements. (Collin dictionary)

Self-defeating. A plan or action that is likely to cause problems or difficulties instead of producing useful results. (Collin dictionary)

Self-deprecating. Criticize one's self or represent themselves as foolish in a light-hearted way. (Collin dictionary)

Self-disclosure. A process of communication by which one person reveals information about themselves to another. (Merriam-Webster Dictionary)

Self- exploration. Taking a look at your own thoughts, feelings, behavior and motivations and asking why. It is looking for the roots of who we are, answers to all the questions we have about ourselves. (Psych center)

Self-Love. The instinct or tendency to seek one's own well-being or to further one's own interest. (Collin dictionary)

Solution-Focused Brief Therapy. Postmodern approach, challenges the basic assumptions of most of the traditional approaches by assuming that there is no single truth and that reality is socially constructed through human interaction. A systemic theory with focus on how people produce their own lives in the context of systems, interactions, social conditioning and discourse. Shifts the focus from problem solving to a complete focus on solutions (Corey, G, 2009 p. 11, 377)

Therapy. The treatment of disease or disorder, as be some remedial, rehabilitating or curative process. (Merriam-Webster Dictionary)

Transference. The displacement of affect from one person to another, the projection of inappropriate emotions onto the leader of group member. Gladding, S.T. (2012).

Triggers. An event, person or situation that makes something else happens. (Merriam-Webster Dictionary)

References

A. Beck, J. S. (2011). Cognitive behavior therapy: Basics and beyond (2nd ed.). New York, NY, US: Guilford Press.

B. Beek, A.T. (1976) Cognitive Therapies & Emotional Disorders. New York: New American Library (p.)

C. Boutot, E.A, Myles, B.S. (2011). Autism Spectrum Disorders. Foundations, Characteristics, and Effective Strategies. Pearson Education, Inc., Upper Saddle River, New Jersey. (p.)

D. Burns, D.D, (2012) Feeling Good: The new mood therapy. New York: New American Library (p.)

E. (Cooper, J. O., Heron, T. E., & Heward, W. L. (2007). Applied Behavior Analysis (2nd Edition) Prentice Hall. (p. 442)

F. Corey, Gerald, (2008) Theory and Practice of Counseling and Psychotherapy (8th Edition). [Brooks/Cole. (p.)

G. Cozby, P. C. (2007). Methods in Behavioral Research (9th Edition) The McGraw. Hill Companies, Higher education. (p.)

H. Crosson-Tower, C. (2008). Understanding Child Abuse and Neglect,7th Edition. Harvest Counseling and Consultation. Pearson (p.)

I. Cully, J.A., & Teten, A.L. 2008. A Therapist's Guide to Brief Cognitive Behavioral Therapy. Department of Veterans Affairs South Central MIRECC, Houston.

J. Durlak, J.A., Furnham, T. and Lampman, C. (1991). Effectiveness of cognitive-behavior therapy for maladapting children: a meta-analysis. Psychological Bulletin 110, 204-214.

K. Durlak, J.A., Furnham, T. and Lampman, C. (1991).; Stallard, P. (2002).

L. Gladding, S.T. (2012). GROUPS, A Counseling Specialty, (6th Edition). Pearson Education, Inc.

M. McKay M & Fleming, P. (2016) Self-Esteem: A Proven Program of Cognitive Techniques for Assessing, Improving & Maintaining Your Self-Esteem. New York: New Harbinger Publications.

N. Miltenberger, R. G., (2008). Behavior Modification. Principles and Procedures (4th Edition). Wadsworth Cengage Learning. (p.)

O. Therapy aid.com

P. Umbreit, J., Ferro J., Liaupsin, C. & Lane, K., (2007) Functional Behavioral Assessment and Function-Based Intervention, An Effective, Practical Approach. Pearson Merrill Prentice Hall. (p.)

Q. Raymond, R. (2015). 12 Signs You Lack Healthy Boundaries (and Why you Need Them). Harley Therapy, April 2, 2015, Counseling, Relationship.

R. Rosenthal, H. (2008) Encyclopedia of Counseling, (3rd Edition). Master Review and Tutorial for the National Counselor Examination, State Counseling Exams and the Counselor Preparation Comprehensive Examination. (p.)

S. Stallard, P. (2002). Think Good-Feel Good.

T. Sue, D.W., and Sue D. (2008). Counseling the Culturally Diverse. Theory and Practice (5th Edition). John Wiley & Sons, Inc. (p.)

U. Stanovich, K. E., (2007). How to Think Straight About Psychology (8th Edition). Allyn and Bacon, Pearson Education, Inc. (p.)

V. Szente, J. Empowering Young Children for Success in School and in Life. *Early Childhood Educ J* **34,** 449–453 (2007). https://doi.org/10.1007/s10643-007-0162-y

Printed in the United States
by Baker & Taylor Publisher Services